TRY THIS!

GREEN & GROSS EXPERIMENTS FOR THE MAD SCIENTIST IN YOU

KAREN ROMANO YOUNG
PHOTOGRAPHS BY MATTHEW RAKOLA

NATIONAL
GEOGRAPHIC

WASHINGTON, D.C.

GREEN&GROSS

It's blooming incredible what you can do in the great outdoors: Grow plants in weird ways. Figure out what organisms eat your leftovers. Tap into the special powers of ordinary fruits and vegetables . . . or eat them.

SEED BOMBS AND SLINGSHOTS

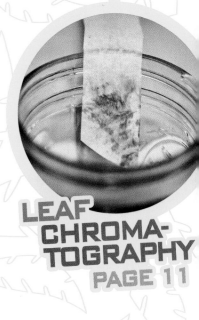

LEAF CHROMA-TOGRAPHY

RAINBOW ROSE

CABBAGE CHECK

SEEDS SPROUT IN WATER BEADS

WHAT DIED?

LEMON-LIT AND POTATO-POWERED LED

GROW YOUR OWN BIOFILM

RAINBOW ROSE

Color a white rose in rainbow shades.

PLANT STRUCTURES AND PROCESSES

HOW LONG IT TAKES
three to four days, including soaking time

WHAT YOU NEED
white rosebud
four small glasses or baby food jars of water
small sharp scissors (such as sewing scissors) or a sharp knife
gel food coloring: red, blue, yellow, violet

NOTE ABOUT FOOD COLORING
This works best with the gel food coloring sold at cake supply shops.

What's a xylem? It's the system of cells inside a plant's roots and stem that transports water from ground or vase to the top of the plant. This project lets you discover what sections of the xylem feed what parts of a blossom.

WHAT TO DO

DAY ONE:

1 USE ONE TEASPOON (5 mL) of gel food coloring: red, blue, yellow, and violet or green. Place one color in each glass or jar, and fill with water only enough to create a thick liquid.

2 CUT YOUR ROSE STEM to six to eight inches (15 to 20 cm) below the bud. Split the stem of the rose into four equal portions. Get the split as even as you can, using small sharp scissors or, with adult assistance, a sharp knife.

3 PLACE ONE PIECE of stem in each of the glasses.

DAYS TWO TO FOUR:

4 LET SOAK. Observe the results.

GLITCH? Your rose won't stand up once the stem is split? Aaliyah used a chopstick and a twist-tie to keep her stem vertical, and rubber-banded the jars together to support the chopstick.

WHAT TO EXPECT Your rose should absorb the colored water through the stem into the petals, resulting in a rainbow rose.

WHAT'S GOING ON? Xylem cells in the plant's stem transport water from the source to the bud. Splitting the stem allows you to see which part of the stem corresponds to which petals in the rose. As the rose absorbs water through the xylem, and the bud opens, the petals take up the food coloring from specific parts of the xylem.

If each petal absorbed water from all parts of the xylem, your rose would be a combination of all of the colors, or brown. You can see that some petals do absorb from more than one part of the xylem, because they appear to be a combination of two of the colors, such as green (blue and yellow) or orange (red and yellow).

QUESTION THIS!

- What accounts for different shades of color?

- What happens if you leave the rose in the dye for longer than four days?

- What happens if you do this with a rose that has a natural color?

- Do different roses absorb color in the same pattern?

SEED BOMBS AND SLINGSHOTS

Make 'em, shoot 'em, grow 'em.

CONCEPTS

PLANTING, SEEDS, PROPULSION

HOW LONG IT TAKES
one or two days, including time spent
soaking seeds and drying seed bombs

WHAT YOU NEED
several packets of seeds
20-pound (9 kg) bag of soil with a loam
or clay component so that it can form a
ball
optional: air-dry clay from a craft store
can be added to help hold the seed
bomb together.
newspaper
optional: compost or peat moss
a baking sheet

ere's a recipe for germination and dissemination. Say what? Make mud pies that provide a growing (germinating) medium for seeds. Then get creative about flinging—or slinging (disseminating)—those seeds out into the environment.

NOTE ABOUT SEEDS
Consider native seeds
that grow easily in your
area, such as wildflowers.
They will grow well and
won't do environmental
damage or alter feeding
habits of native insects
and birds.

WHAT TO DO

DAY ONE:

1 COVER OR FILL the baking sheet with newspaper. This is your drying rack.

2 SOAK THE SEEDS in water for one to eight hours. Adding compost or peat moss to this water will make it more nutritious for the seeds.

3 MIX THE SOIL with your hands until it holds together in a ball. (Adding air-dry clay may help.) Make table-tennis-size balls of soil.

4 SET EACH SEED BALL on newspaper and let them dry for several hours or overnight.

DAY TWO:

5 PLANT YOUR SEED BALLS by hand, or throw, catapult, or slingshot them into a plowed or dug-over garden or field.

> **WHAT TO EXPECT** Plants will grow in a random, scattered pattern and won't look like a formal garden.

> **WHAT'S GOING ON?** Seed balls maintain seeds in a good condition for growing. Mixing the seeds with compost, peat moss, and nutritious soil keeps them in a state that fosters healthy plants that may grow more quickly.

QUESTION THIS!

• How would you design an experiment that would test whether seed balls are a beneficial way to plant compared with sowing dry seeds?

• Seed bombs are a quick way to plant seeds in vacant lots or along the highway. Why do you think some people use them for this purpose?

WHAT TO DO

1 USE YOUR PARING knife to carve a light groove an inch from the top of each branch of the Y. This will help your sling stay in place when you attach it.

2 FOR THE SADDLE: Cut a piece of leather or fabric about 3½ inches by 2 inches (8.9 x 5.1 cm). This will be the saddle. (The seed bomb rides in it.) Cut a hole in each end big enough to accommodate the surgical tubing.

3 THREAD ONE PIECE of surgical tubing 1½ inches (3.8 cm) through one hole in the saddle. Double it over and use dental floss to tie it, then wind the floss around the joint about five times and knot it again. Do the same with the other piece of tubing and the other end of the saddle.

4 ATTACH THE FREE end of each piece of tubing to the branches of the Y-stick. Wrap the end around the stick, leaving a tail 1½ inches (3.8 cm) long, and fasten it with the dental floss as you did before. Now do the same with the other branch.

WHAT TO EXPECT You'll have a slingshot with a saddle wide enough to hold a seed bomb. Load a seed bomb into the saddle, pull it back, aim well, and release.

WHAT'S HAPPENING? When you fire a slingshot, pulling back the elastic surgical tubing, the energy of your pull is stored in the elastic fibers and transferred to the seed bomb to release quickly.

GLITCH? If your seed bomb falls apart while it flies out of the slingshot, experiment a little with its consistency. It may need to be dried more to harden it, or wetted again slightly to help it hold together. Consider freezing your seed balls before firing them. You might get them to fly farther, and they'll thaw quickly once they land.

BONUS: SEED BOMB SLINGSHOT

WHAT YOU NEED
a Y-shaped stick. Look for a branch about an inch thick.
two 12-inch (30.5 cm) pieces of surgical tubing
dental floss
leather, upholstery fabric, or denim (your old jeans will work fine)
scissors
a paring knife

NOTE ABOUT Y-STICKS Some people say that microwaving the Y-stick for 30 seconds will toughen it up, but Niyanna and Bailey didn't bother with this. Theirs worked fine without it.

CABBAGE CHECK

Who knew cabbage had special powers?

CONCEPTS

ACIDS AND BASES, PH SCALE
INDICATORS

>> **HOW LONG IT TAKES**
one hour

> **WHAT YOU NEED**
red cabbage, cut into big chunks
pot to hold the cabbage
water
stove
optional: juicer
three clear glasses or jars
lemon juice or vinegar (acids)
toothpaste or baking soda (sodium
bicarbonate) (bases)
optional: ammonia, other kitchen
substances

W hat's a pH indicator? The pH scale has acid on one end and base on the other. A pH indicator is a substance that will change colors when combined with something to show whether that something is a base or an acid.

CABBAGE CHECK
(CONTINUED)

NOTE ABOUT CABBAGE JUICE
The purpose of the first two steps is to get the cabbage juice to experiment with. If you have a juicer, you can use that instead of boiling the cabbage. The juice you get should be purple.

WHAT TO DO

1 PLACE THE CABBAGE in the pot and cover it with water. With adult supervision, heat the pot until the water boils for five minutes. Let cool.

2 DRAIN THE WATER and keep it. Notice the color of the water.

3 DIVIDE THE CABBAGE water into three different glasses or jars.

4 ADD LEMON JUICE or vinegar to one glass. What happens to the color of the water?

5 ADD TOOTHPASTE or baking soda to another glass. What happens to the color of the water?

WHAT TO EXPECT The cabbage water should be purple. Adding acid should turn it red or pink. Adding base or alkali should turn it green.

WHAT'S GOING ON? The coloring in the cabbage juice is a pH indicator, which turns red when it is added to an acid and blue-green when added to a base.

"Fuchsia . . . milky . . . light purple . . . turquoise. . . berry color . . . bubbly . . . neutral . . . forest green."

—Emily

QUESTION THIS!

• What can you add to the leftover cup that might change its color? Isaac and Emily tried some other items found around the kitchen, including soda and peanut butter.

LEAF CHROMA-TOGRAPHY

What color does a leaf leave?

>> **HOW LONG IT TAKES**
one hour

>> **WHAT YOU NEED**
leaves
four clear glasses or jars
four pencils
transparent tape
water
rubbing alcohol
coffee filters (you can also use chromatography paper, available from a science supply store, but you don't need to)
scissors
coin

What's chromatography? It's a set of lab activities that separates mixtures—in this case, the pigments that work together to make the color of a leaf.

NOTE ABOUT LEAVES
It's great to do this in autumn in a location with colorful falling leaves, but you can also use spinach leaves or other vegetable leaves, and red maple has a great effect even when the leaves are still green.

LEAF CHROMA-TOGRAPHY
(CONTINUED)

WHAT TO DO

1 GATHER leaves.

2 CUT THE COFFEE filter paper into four strips six inches (15 cm) long and one inch (2.5 cm) wide. Cut one end of the strip to a point.

3 PLACE A LEAF on the paper ¼ inch (.64 cm) below the pointed end. Rub a coin over the leaf to scrape it so that its juice goes into the paper. Do this with the three other leaves and strips of paper.

4 TAPE THE UNPOINTED end of each paper strip to the middle of a pencil. Roll the strip around the pencil.

5 POUR ABOUT ¼ inch (.64 cm) of rubbing alcohol into each jar.

6 SET EACH PENCIL across the mouth of a jar. Carefully unroll the paper so that only the point of the strip touches the alcohol.

7 OBSERVE what happens as the alcohol is absorbed up the paper, moving the pigments (substances causing colors) up the paper. It should take 15 minutes or so for the colors to separate. Take the paper out of the alcohol before the pigments reach the top of the paper.

WHAT TO EXPECT Colors will appear on the paper, some in bands of color.

WHAT'S GOING ON? The green of the leaf (chlorophyll) and other pigments such as carotene (orange) or xanthophyll (yellow) may appear.

GLITCH? Jason and Allison advise: Keep an eye on this one, because if you leave it too long, the color may disappear.

QUESTION THIS!

• What pigments do you think you would observe from different kinds of leaves?

• What's the difference between leaves that are changing with autumn and those that are still green?

LEMON-LIT AND POTATO-POWERED LED

We found this one challenging, to say the least.

ELECTRICITY, CURRENT, VOLTAGE, ACIDS, BATTERIES

> **POTATO-POWERED LED #1:**
> **HOW LONG IT TAKES**
> twenty minutes (to start with) plus
> tinkering time
> Note: We spent at least a week on this
> in the end.

> **WHAT YOU NEED**
> For this experiment:
> potatoes
> two zinc (galvanized) nails
> two pennies
> an LED
> about a yard of copper wire
> paring knife
> optional: electrical tape
>
> For the rest of the light/potato/
> lemon attempts in this book:
> potatoes
> lemons
> pennies minted before 1982 (they have
> copper)
> a coil of copper wire
> zinc (galvanized) nails
> test leads (we ended up using about
> 30)
> an LED
> hot pepper sauce
> copper wool (like steel wool, but made
> from copper)

hat is an LED? LED stands for light-emitting diode. An LED contains semi-conducting material and uses electricity to light. LEDs are different from incandescent bulbs with filaments that burn out, in that they light because electrons move through semiconductor material inside them.

LEMON-LIT AND POTATO-POWERED LED

WHAT TO DO

FOR THIS EXPERIMENT:

1 CUT ONE potato in half.

2 WRAP AN 18-INCH (46-cm) piece of wire five or six times around the penny, leaving a tail.

3 USE THE KNIFE to make a slot in each potato that will allow a penny to slide in almost all the way, leaving the tail outside. Insert the pennies into the slots.

4 WIND WIRE AROUND each nail. Push one nail into each potato half, about two inches (5.1 cm) from the penny. Don't let the nail and penny touch.

5 USE THE WIRE from one penny to attach to the nail on the other potato.

6 USE THE WIRE from the other penny and the wire from the other nail to connect to the LED.

7 USE THE WIRE from the nail (the cathode, or negative electrode) to attach to the positive connector (the longer wire) on the LED. To do this, wind or hook the potato wire and the LED wire together.

8 USE THE WIRE from the nail (the anode, or positive electrode) to attach to the negative connector (the shorter wire) on the LED. If you wish, use electrical tape to fasten the connections tightly.

> FAIL! The LED didn't light. The Internet says lemons work even better. Let's try them instead.

LEMON-LIT LED #2: Rig one lemon. using copper pennies. zinc nails. and copper wire.

WHAT DID WE CHANGE?
1. We used a lemon instead of potato halves. We used it whole. not cutting it in half.

FAIL! The LED still didn't light. Was the wiring the problem? Since we were not trying to assess how well we wired, we were trying to assess if a lemon could light an LED, we decided to revise the plan.

"But it's not working!"
—Aaliyah

For the rest of the attempts, turn the page.

NOTE ABOUT THE LEMON/ POTATO/LED PROJECTS Warning! Proceed at your own risk. No, it's not dangerous—unless you're worried about going bonkers.

Why? This one doesn't work. Or maybe I should say it wouldn't work, or maybe couldn't work the way we were doing it. The fact is that we ended up trying it all kinds of ways and it just never did work. Epic Fail! Or was it?

POTATO-POWERED LED #2: We used one potato halved, plus test leads instead of copper wire.

WHAT DID WE CHANGE?
1. Emily went back to the potatoes for another try.
2. She got rid of the copper wires wrapped around the pennies and nails and used the alligator clips on the test leads to create the connections instead.

FAIL! Maybe the problem was that the pennies were too dirty. We made a big effort to find pre-1982 pennies, soaked them in hot pepper sauce to remove the oxidation and scrubbed them with copper wool to shine them even more. But maybe the pennies didn't have enough copper in them.

LEMON-LIT LED #2: We used one lemon, with copper wire instead of pennies, and test leads.

WHAT DID WE CHANGE?
Sossi and Trijon went back to the lemons for another try, using the test leads instead.

FAIL! Maybe the whole thing was working just fine, but without a voltmeter, we couldn't check how much voltage we were generating. You can try a voltmeter with your project, but we didn't go that far. We figured we just needed more of a good thing—more lemon power to light our LED. We thought we could do this if we wired together a bunch of lemon or potato "batteries."

POTATO-POWERED LED #3: We used multiple potatoes, linked in series.

WHAT DID WE CHANGE?
1. We tried the potatoes again.
2. We linked a bunch of potatoes in series, using test leads to connect anode (positive electrode: pennies) to cathode (negative electrode: nails), and using the last nail on one end and the last penny on the other end to connect with the LED.

FAIL! Linking in series made it a big battery that should have had lots of voltage, but since it still didn't light the LED, we wondered if we needed to improve how much current we were generating, not just voltage. We tried wiring in such a way that would increase current as well as voltage—linking in parallel as well as in series.

LEMON-LIT LED #3: We used multiple lemons, linked in series and in parallel.

WHAT DID WE CHANGE?
1. We went back to the lemons again.
2. Instead of just linking the lemons in series, we linked them in parallel, too. So each penny had two test leads, one connecting it to the nail on the next lemon, and the other connecting it to the penny on the next lemon. Each nail had two test leads, one connecting it to the penny on the next lemon, and the other connecting it to the nail on the next lemon. The last penny on one end and the last nail on the other end had test leads connecting to the LED.

FAIL! After linking together ten lemons in series and in parallel, and a large number of potato halves, too, we have had enough of this experiment. We've learned some important things about circuitry, wiring, current, and voltage, and we've already learned to distrust some things we see on the Internet. Yes, it could certainly be our mistake. Those lemons and spuds could be chock-full of energy. But we're going to move on, turning our energy to a different experiment. Maybe if we give the lemons and potatoes a break, the "light" will finally turn on and we'll realize what we've been doing wrong the whole time.

SEEDS SPROUT IN WATER BEADS

6

Like watching seeds grow—because you can actually see it happening!

CONCEPTS

SEED GERMINATION, PROPERTIES OF POLYMERS, PRINCIPLES OF WATER

HOW LONG IT TAKES
one to four days, including germination time for the seeds

WHAT YOU NEED
water beads (seed beads or ready-made ones that have already absorbed water)
seeds
water
a shallow container with a clear lid
optional: pointed knife

f you were a seed, where would you want to germinate? If not in a warm pot of soil, why not a bubble of water of your very own?

NOTE ABOUT WATER BEADS
These tiny beads made of acrylic polymer will absorb nearly 100 times their weight in water when soaked, and will become large and gel-like.

NOTE ABOUT SEEDS
Small, flat, and pointy seeds work best for this project. Consider zinnias and marigolds, which germinate easily and are sharp enough to pierce the water beads.

WHAT TO DO

DAY ONE:

1 MAKE WATER BEADS.
Add water to seed beads and let them soak, or use ready-made ones. Place the water beads in a shallow container.

2 USE A SEED or the point of a knife to start a slit in the water bead.

3 INSERT THE SEED as far as you can into the water bead, trying not to split the bead. If you do split it, start over with another bead.

4 PLACE BEADS in the container. Pour water in among the beads, and keep them wet as the seeds germinate.

5 COVER THE CONTAINER with the lid and set it in a bright spot.

DAYS TWO TO FOUR:

6 CHECK your seeds daily to see how they're doing.

WHAT TO EXPECT Your seeds should germinate in three or four days. You can watch the process through the clear water bead.

WHAT'S HAPPENING? The clear polymer feeds water to the seed, which absorbs it and grows in full view. The water bead also acts as an insulator for the seed, helping maximize sun and heat.

BONUS

PLANT YOUR WATER BEADS

What happens?

QUESTION THIS!

• What would happen to the seed if you let the water bead dry out?

"The water beads let you see all the parts of the seed."
—Priyanka

GROW YOUR OWN BIOFILM

Soup + dirt + warmth = biofilm

CONCEPTS

MICROBIAL BIOLOGY, DECOMPOSITION

HOW LONG IT TAKES
three days to one week

WHAT YOU NEED
a cup (.25 L) of soup (low-sodium chicken soup works best)
pinch of dirt
food coloring
water
plastic container
measuring cup

What's biofilm? It's a colony of bacteria that forms on a surface—a pond, a bowl, a boat in the ocean. The bacteria form a thin film, spreading out to make the most of the food source. Biofilm is also known as scum or slime.

NOTE ABOUT BIOFILM
If it smells awful, you've probably met your goal of achieving biofilm.

WHAT TO DO

DAY ONE:

1 POUR A CUP (.25 L) **OF SOUP** into the container and add the dirt.

2 LEAVE THE CONTAINER in a warm place, uncovered, for four to five days. The ideal temperature is 98.6°F (37°C)—body temperature. You may need to leave it out longer if it's cooler.

DAYS TWO AND ON:

3 WATCH FOR A CHANGE in the liquid. When it begins to cloud, biofilm is forming.

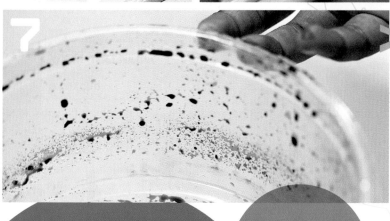

LAST DAY:

4 DUMP OUT THE LIQUID

and gently rinse the container with water. No scrubbing. No soap.

5 DRIP THE FOOD coloring

down the inside walls of the container. Swirl it around to coat the bottom and sides. Wait 15 minutes, swirling the color again every few minutes.

6 FILL THE CONTAINER with

water, then dump out the colored water.

7 THE SMALL SPOTS of color

on the walls of the container are the biofilm.

WHAT TO EXPECT The biofilm will form a ring around the container. It will be difficult to rinse it from the container even with soap, water, and some scrubbing.

WHAT'S GOING ON? Bacteria are tiny organisms that live in two ways: motile (moving freely) and sessile (in a group on a surface). Some motile bacteria become sessile, settling down near a food source that can keep them fed even if they quit moving. A biofilm is a colony of bacteria that live on a surface. If you provide bacteria with a food source, a biofilm may form.

The dirt provided the start-up for the biofilm. One teaspoon (5 mL) of dirt can harbor between 100 million and 1 billion bacteria. In the container, bacteria grow best at the boundary of air and liquid.

OUR TRY

It was a hot week, and we put our chicken broth/dirt concoction in an attic closet with no air conditioning. It only took 48 hours for a beautiful biofilm to form. Success! Janelle and Dylan can confirm that it sure had a strong smell.

"Can we get this out of here now? It stinks!"
—Lori

QUESTION THIS!

• What role does the chicken soup play?

• What do biofilms do when they form in liquids in nature?

• Are there other invisible biofilms in liquids around the house?

WHAT DIED?

What comes to get food that's left out?

CONCEPTS

DECOMPOSITION, MICROBIOLOGY, DECAY,
ORGANIC MATERIALS, BACTERIA,
INSECTS, CORPSE FAUNA

HOW LONG IT TAKES
two to four days, possibly longer in cold
weather

WHAT YOU NEED
food samples
containers
outdoor thermometer
magnifying lens
dissecting microscope
bug identification guides
optional: camera, smartphone, or video
camera

f you leave food out, SOMETHING
will come to live on it or lay eggs
on it. In this observation, discover
what arrives to make the most of
your leftovers.

WHAT TO DO

DAY ONE:

1 WORK IN AN OPEN-AIR area, compost heap, or compost bin—a place that is open to bugs but not birds or other animals.

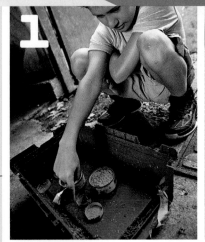

2 SET UP FOUR containers with a small sample of food inside each. If you want, these samples can represent the four food groups: vegetable/fruit, meat/fish, bread/grains, and milk/dairy.

DAYS TWO TO FOUR:

3 KEEP A CAREFUL record of what you observe through your senses. Each day, record the temperature in the area where your samples are. Note whether you can see signs that bugs or other creatures have been attracted to your samples, including any film or mold that forms. You may want to photograph the samples every day to compare them.

4 EVERY ONE OR TWO days (decide which interval you want to study), remove the samples from the containers to examine them with a magnifying lens and microscope. Count, try to identify, and sketch the bugs and other life forms that colonize each sample. Add descriptions to your notes, including sensory observations: texture, color, and smell—but not taste!

WHAT TO EXPECT You may see mold, biofilm or scum, bugs, worms, flies, and so on.

WHAT'S GOING ON? Nature abhors a vacuum. If there is food, something will come to eat it.

OUR TRY

We put out duplicate food—chicken broth, blackberry jam, and cat food—every other day for six days. We set out the food in the yard, in a cat carrier with a brick on top, but that didn't stop coyotes from pulling it apart and getting the food on the second night. After that we replaced the food and kept the cat carrier in the garage, where flies could still get to it. After we opened it to see what we had and examine it with the microscope, we dumped the cat carrier near the compost heap—and later, we had a glorious infestation of beetles.

"The maggots look like moving white noodles."
—Luke

QUESTION THIS!

• What would happen to this food if nothing were able to reach it?

• What would happen to this food if you let more time pass?

CREDITS

Acknowledgments

Our Models: Aaliyah, Abigail, Adriana, Allison, Ariel, Bailey, Brandon, Caitlyn, Cole, Doug, Dylan, Emily, Isaac, Janelle, Jarrett, Jason, Jen, Justin, Lori, Luke, Mae, Marco, Nick, Nikitha, Niyanna, Patsy, Priyanka, Serenity, Sossi, Stephanie, Trijon, Wyatt

Special thanks to Tina Kiniry at the John Casablancas Modeling Agency

All photographs shot on location by Matthew Rakola

Published by the National Geographic Society

John M. Fahey, *Chairman of the Board and Chief Executive Officer*
Declan Moore, *Executive Vice President; President, Publishing and Travel*
Melina Gerosa Bellows, *Executive Vice President; Chief Creative Officer, Books, Kids, and Family*

Prepared by the Book Division

Hector Sierra, *Senior Vice President and General Manager*
Nancy Laties Feresten, *Senior Vice President, Kids Publishing and Media*
Jennifer Emmett, *Vice President, Editorial Director, Kids Books*
Eva Absher-Schantz, *Design Director, Kids Publishing and Media*
Jay Sumner, *Director of Photography, Kids Publishing and Media*
R. Gary Colbert, *Production Director*
Jennifer A. Thornton, *Director of Managing Editorial*

Staff for This Book

Priyanka Lamichhane, *Project Editor*
Angela Modany, *Assistant Editor*
Eva Absher-Schantz, *Art Director*
Lori Epstein, *Senior Photo Editor*
Itzhack Shelomi, *Designer*
Ariane Szu-Tu, *Editorial Assistant*
Paige Towler, *Editorial Intern*
Sanjida Rashid and Rachel Kenny, *Design Production Assistants*
Margaret Leist, *Photo Assistant*
Grace Hill, *Associate Managing Editor*
Joan Gossett, *Production Editor*
Lewis R. Bassford, *Production Manager*
Susan Borke, *Legal and Business Affairs*

Production Services

Phillip L. Schlosser, *Senior Vice President*
Chris Brown, *Vice President, NG Book Manufacturing*
George Bounelis, *Senior Production Manager*
Nicole Elliott, *Director of Production*
Rachel Faulise, *Manager*
Robert L. Barr, *Manager*

The National Geographic Society is one of the world's largest nonprofit scientific and educational organizations. Founded in 1888 to "increase and diffuse geographic knowledge," the Society's mission is to inspire people to care about the planet. It reaches more than 400 million people worldwide each month through its official journal, *National Geographic*, and other magazines; National Geographic Channel; television documentaries; music; radio; films; books; DVDs; maps; exhibitions; live events; school publishing programs; interactive media; and merchandise. National Geographic has funded more than 10,000 scientific research, conservation and exploration projects and supports an education program promoting geographic literacy.

For more information, please visit nationalgeographic.com, call 1-800-NGS LINE (647-5463), or write to the following address:

National Geographic Society
1145 17th Street N.W.
Washington, D.C. 20036-4688 U.S.A.

Visit us online at nationalgeographic.com/books

For librarians and teachers: ngchildrensbooks.org

More for kids from National Geographic:
kids.nationalgeographic.com

For information about special discounts for bulk purchases, please contact National Geographic Books Special Sales: ngspecsales@ngs.org

For rights or permissions inquiries, please contact National Geographic Books Subsidiary Rights: ngbookrights@ngs.org

Dollar Tree edition ISBN: 978-1-4263-2380-5

Printed in the U.S.A.
15/KG/1

All content and information published in this book is provided to the reader "as is" and without any warranties. While the experiments in this book should be safe as conducted and instructed, they still carry inherent risks and hazards. The author, photographer, and publisher specifically disclaim all responsibility for any injury, loss, or damage caused or sustained while performing any of the experiments in this book. We strongly recommend adult supervision and following proper safety precautions when conducting any of these experiments.